ORPHEUS & EURYDICE

ORPHEUS & EURYDICE

A Lyric Sequence

Gregory Orr

COPPER CANYON PRESS

ACKNOWLEDGMENTS

Versions of some of these poems have appeared in the following magazines: *Artful Dodge, Atlanta Review, Ploughshares,* and the on-line magazine *Slate.*

Printed in the United States of America.

Copper Canyon Press gratefully acknowledges Kathy Muehlemann for the use of her painting *Monk's Yellow Dream* on the cover, and Nellie Bridge for the use of her drawings on the cover and in the interior of this book.

Copper Canyon Press is in residence under the auspices of the Centrum Foundation at Fort Worden State Park in Port Townsend, Washington. Centrum sponsors artist residencies, education workshops for Washington State students and teachers, blues, jazz, and fiddle tunes festivals, classical music performances, and The Port Townsend Writers' Conference.

LIBRARY OF CONGRESS CATALOGING-IN-PUBLICATION DATA
Orr, Gregory.
Orpheus and Eurydice: a lyric sequence / by Gregory Orr.
   p. cm.
ISBN 1-55659-151-9
1. Orpheus (Greek mythology) – Poetry. 2. Eurydice (Greek mythology) – Poetry. I. Title.
PS3565.R7 O77 2001
811'.54 – DC21   00-010242
CIP

COPPER CANYON PRESS

Post Office Box 271
Port Townsend, Washington 98368
www.coppercanyonpress.org

Contents

It's winter…

Fields took on…

How can I celebrate love,
now that I know what it does?

ORPHEUS & EURYDICE

The Entrance to the Underworld

A common enough mistake:
looking in the wrong place.
It's not a fissure
in the earth, or crack
in a cliff face
that leads sharply down.

You were looking in the wrong
world. It was inside
you – entrance
to that cavern
deeper than hell,
more dark and lonely.
Didn't you feel it open
at her first touch?

When I first saw...

When I first saw her
she was so beautiful
I wanted to be a mirror
and hold all of her.
My eyes couldn't do that,
much as I tried
to calm them, saying:
"Drink deep of her face."

If I had become a lake...
A mirror is all surface
but a lake has depths.
I would have drawn her in,
undine or water nymph,
alive inside me.

Is this what...

Is this what it's like
to be born:
to be torn asunder?

My green leaves burn,
pale and splintered
inner wood;
            deep cleft
lightning made.

We've come...

ORPHEUS

Calm now, curled away
from each other, backs
just touching, we've come
full circle
to that awkward
primordial creature:
man and woman
as a single animal
joined at the base of the spine.

In the Meadow

EURYDICE

Marble pillars
of palace
or temple –
so what?
I've seen them
tumbled by vines.

And our beautiful
bodies –
how long
will they last?

Shallow valley
where we
lie down,
crushing a circle
in tall grass.

Above it
the gods
drift
on low clouds,
letting down
bright lines

of sunlight
with tiny
golden hooks.

In my dream...

In my dream, she was tired
and lay down at the foot
of the hill.

       I climbed on,
eager to walk in the summit's
wind-tossed grasses
that blazed up in last light.

But when I got there, the sun
was gone and the wind
so cold it seemed
to blow right through me.

I turned to her and called
but she was asleep
in the hill's shadow
which she had become.

A snake...

A snake no bigger
than a bracelet
of braided gold
unfastened and cast aside
in the haste of love…

The bite itself – only
the pinprick
you might feel
stepping barefoot
on the open clasp.

His Lament

How is it she lies here,
her body still
so warm it makes me wince?

How is it she's nothing now?

They say there's a god
who can squeeze mud
in his fist
breathe on it and it lives.

And me? All I do is kneel
beside her corpse,
numbly repeating her name
as if
some nacreous alchemy
of the voice
could pearl a piece of dust.

Loss...

Loss more than leaves
fallen, more than green
gone. Loss past grieving.

Though roots probe
and branches grope outward
into empty air, she's
vanished past
finding, whose loss
is carved in bark, in bone.

If...

*If your gaze takes in
the world,
a person's a puny thing.*

*If a person is all
you see,
the rest falls away
and she becomes the world.*

*But there's another world
into which a person
can disappear.*

*Then what remains?
Only your word for her:
Eurydice.*

When I was alive...

When I was alive – only glimpses,
moments of bliss but
always the body resisting,
refusing to let
the soul go.

        In that world
I was a fish too eager
to enter the nets; here,
I'm a river.

        There, I was a bird
hopelessly searching for its nest;
here, I'm a wind that blows
where it wishes and needs no rest.

When I died, all Orpheus heard
was a small, ambiguous cry.
How could he know how free I felt
as I unwound the long bandage
of my skin and stepped out?

She paused...

On the path down,
she paused at the stone
gates and saw
a story like hers
carved there:

the child Persephone,
fleeing the dark god,
stumbles.
          Her head's
thrown back, its sunburst
of curls – a golden
chrysanthemum
snapped from its stalk.
Even as she falls
a crack appears
beneath her feet.

The moral's clear:
a mortal's a blossom
the earth opens for.

Orpheus Descending

Before we lay together
in the fragrant
grass
I was only
half alive.

A frost came
and scythed
the whole
field flat.

Maybe she loved me,
maybe not –
who knows?
Not even the gods
can see into
a human heart –
it's that dark.

But mine beats
its syllables
of need
and I begin
my journey

with no thought
but this:

        I'm lost,
lost,
unless I bring her back.

I was moving...

I was moving down the bank
toward the boat, lost
in the mob of newly dead,
when scowling Charon
stepped from the mist
to grab me by my shoulder:
"You'll go no farther
till you're dead."

I thought: What's music
to a brute like this,
and yet the chord I struck
hit him like a blow.
His face softened.
He sat down right there
in the stinking mud,
chin propped on fists, listening.

When Eurydice saw him

When Eurydice saw him
huddled in a thick cloak,
she should have known
he was alive,
the way he shivered
beneath its useless folds.

But what she saw
was the usual: a stranger
confused in a new world.
And when she touched him
on the shoulder,
it was nothing
personal, a kindness
he misunderstood.
To guide someone
through the halls of hell
is not the same as love.

Look, they descend

Look, they descend:
light, water,
all things
released
seek the earth.

Why should you
resist
so insistently?
Pushing away
with each step,
you only postpone.

All things go
downward.
Even the rocks
settle and sink,
even the flowers bow.

Orpheus stood in the dark...

Orpheus stood
in the dark hall
and, with his hands
on the strings
and his sung words,
tried to conjure
her body
out of empty air.

All the while,
Eurydice
was standing
behind him.
He only had to turn
and she was there.

The Ghosts Listen to Orpheus Sing

He stood before the throne
and we stared, astonished,
at his breath pluming
in the cold air.

And then he strummed
his lyre and sang
the things we knew
and had forgot –
the earth in all its seasons
but especially spring
whose kiss melts
the icicle's bone
so that the dead bush
blooms again.

He sang the splendid wings
sex lends.

He sang the years passing
like sparks
flung in the dark:
anvil, tongs, and hammer
toiling at pleasure's forge.

Last of all it was loss
he sang, how like a vine
it climbs the wall,
sends roots and tendrils
inward,
bringing to the heart
of the hardest stone
the deep bursting emptiness of song.

My body was never marred

My body was never marred;
no dart of Eros
ever pierced my skin.
Where my heart was
a pomegranate is —
how could I be moved?

And yet, as he sang,
I watched pale faces
in our hall of ghosts
swaying like a meadow
and memory blossomed.
I saw again
my lost companions
wandering in sunlight
in the upper air.
I walked among them
green and careless,
not hearing the rhythm
of his chariot approaching,
not yet caught
in the sickle
of his arm's curve.

At the field's edge
I searched for lilies;
never saw the god
whom love had ravaged,
myself the flower
he'd come to gather.

Because I sensed

Because I sensed
that love in hell
was a cold thing,
a coupling of statues
(no grimace twisting
features, no moan
escaping lips),
I conjured Aphrodite,
goddess of desire.

Before their eyes
she stepped
from shell to shore
in all her naked glory.
And as she walked
among them
my syllables praised
her emblems,
praised
the leafy threshold
and the golden bone,
praised even
her softest kiss
that turns

the thickest skin
inside out
till it becomes
all nerve,
all tingle and cringe.

It hurt me to hear...

HADES

It hurt me to hear my subjects –
nothing but ghosts, nothing
but gray husks – groaning aloud.

His songs that blended anguish
and desire made their brows furrow,
their placid faces lose all repose.

In my dark realm, music's painful
as first light to sleeping eyes:
white line above black trees,
dawn's chalk scraped across the board.

When they said...

EURYDICE

When they said I must leave hell
and I put on flesh again,
it felt like a soiled dress.

And as I followed him
up the steep path
I kept staring at his feet,
callused, bleeding. How
could I once have held
and kissed them?

           My sandal
came undone. I paused
for breath because
air hurt my lungs.

A hundred delays offered
their help, their hope,
but still the opening
grew until at last I saw
his body silhouetted
against the entrance glare:
dark pupil
of an eye that stared.

In the cave mouth...

In the cave mouth I stopped,
stunned, to lean against
a broken limestone tooth.

The light was like a wall
and I was afraid.
I turned to her as I had before:

to save myself.

She was something between
the abyss and me,
something my eyes could cling to.

Once the two of us

Once the two of us
were a single stream
flowing over
and around itself
as if our bodies
had no bounds
but were only
a liquid braiding
of currents
and sensuous eddies.

Now I watch her
pale form flee alone
back down
the precipitous path.
She's a waterfall
plunging over the lip
of a cliff:

　　　white foam
shattering on the rocks below.

It's winter...

It's winter. Wind gnaws
a bone sky.
The sap has sunk.
Stiff and numb, I
no longer feel.

Spring is long gone,
when crocuses poked
their green tongues
up through mud
and a warm wind
rubbed each bud
between its thumb
and finger.

                What
keeps me here?
Only my heart
that won't give up —
a puffed sparrow
gripping a twig,
a stubborn
leaf in a bare shrub.

In the shadows...

In the shadows at the clearing's
edge, wounded deer stood
and wild boar gored with spears
but not brought down,
and other animals, smaller,
whimpering among the branches.

One of them stepped forward,
approached the spot where Orpheus
was seated alone on a boulder.

It was a fox who, having caught
his paw in a trap,
had chewed it off.

               Bowing,
he said: "Enough
of maiming and blame.
We want to be lifted up
in song, our lost limbs
restored.

        Orpheus,
she was you in another body.
Bright threads bound you together.

Rise now and strike your lyre.
Sing what connects us,
what no tooth can sever."

His Grief

With my words
I'll make rocks
weep and trees
toss down
their branches
in despair.

In its heart
each object
guards a tear
so round
and absolute
it mirrors all
the passing scene.
Those clear globes
are the souls
of things.
I want to shatter
them. I want
to make them sing.

Far below, plowed fields...

Far below, plowed fields vibrated
in the spring heat like black harps.

But all that was behind him now:
the lakes and swamps, the low places,
the lilacs with their heart-shaped
leaves shading the clustered huts.

He turned to the windy cliffs
and pathless slopes above the tree line
where each boulder gave forth
its single, inconsolable note.

Who knows? Maybe it would be simpler.
When she was alive, her body
confused him; he couldn't think
clearly when she was close. Scent
of her skin made him dizzy.

Now, where she had been: only
a gaping hole in air,
an emptiness he could fill with song.

The Wedge

When there were two of us
there was one world

and one moon. When you
died, I was alone

in another world
whose two moons

of grief and rage
wax and wane

in the starless sky.
By their light,

all I eat becomes
ashes on my tongue.

Now I can't stand
to be touched

or to see anyone
touching. When I find

lovers, I set
this wedge between them:

love is no use,
though lovers are used;

who seeks to soothe
will only bruise.

The Maenads

The maenads came to me,
demanding I praise
the loveliest among them.

As if I would when none
had her eyes, their hue:
blue of lapis, a glacial

blue, blue of the worm
that gnaws the heart
till the heart is gnawed through.

Warned his song...

Warned his song could tame
our frenzy, we notched
our clamor higher and trapped
him on the riverbank.

The rest was easy. A body
comes apart like a straw doll
if enough of us tug and pull
(though, oddly, none
could mar his face or tear
those lips that mocked us).

And then we were spent
and a silence fell
upon our group.
           I lifted
his beautiful head
and threw it in the river
but it would not sink.

By the Shore

Some of the women knelt
on the muddy shore,
rinsing his blood
from their limbs.

Others stood in a daze,
gazing off downriver
where the singing head
had long since disappeared.

The birds were silent
and even the river had stopped
its river sound, and no
breeze stirred the leaves.

Everything had lost its voice
and listened now inside,
listened to Orpheus.

His Dream: The Black Tree/Thirst

I saw her, out past the first
waves, swaying
on an undulant stalk.

At my feet, she'd left
her wisdom and bones –
unsortable pile on the shore.

Then I was under a tree,
its trunk twined
with a thick helix of vine,
a twinned upthrusting,
its intermingled foliage
more green than black.

Stepping from the dark,
she held cupped hands
to my lips.
          "Everything
is risk," she whispered.
"If you doubt, it becomes
sand trickling
through skeletal fingers.
Believe, and it's water
from what deep well."

Tomb of Orpheus

My limbs were scattered.
Wild animals ate
my flesh. My bones
lay unburied.
None of that matters.

Death is a rock
tossed in a river –
as soon as they open
your wounds close.

When I was alive
the best of me
was only mud
and took
the impress of her.

Still I remember
and murmur her name.
My song is the fossil;
she was the fern.

Fields took on...

Fields took on their final
green; the sea was still
as the sky.

         No longer
did clouds drift
toward the horizon
like shadows without bodies,
or like wings
without that
which they were meant to lift.

And the rose, whose rich
petals are saturated
with vanishing...

ABOUT THE AUTHOR

Gregory Orr is the author of six previous poetry books and three books of criticism. He teaches at the University of Virginia and lives with his wife and daughters in Charlottesville.

BOOKS BY GREGORY ORR

POETRY

City of Salt (University of Pittsburgh Press, 1995)
New & Selected Poems (Wesleyan University Press, 1988)
We Must Make a Kingdom of It (Wesleyan University Press, 1986)
The Red House (Harper & Row, 1980)
Gathering the Bones Together (Harper & Row, 1975)
Burning the Empty Nests (Harper & Row, 1973)

CRITICISM

Poets Teaching Poets: Self and the World (edited by Voigt and Orr,
    University of Michigan Press, 1996)
Richer Entanglements: Essays and Notes on Poetry and Poems
    (University of Michigan Press, 1993)
Stanley Kunitz: An Introduction to the Poetry (Columbia University
    Press, 1985)

The book is set in Electra, created
by American typographer and book
designer W.A. Dwiggins in 1935, with
titles set in ITC Tyfa™, designed by
Czech designer Josef Tyfa in 1959
and inspired by the forms of modern
architecture. Book design and
composition by VJB/Scribe.